Operation Mincemeat

A Captivating Guide to the Daring Deception That Changed the Course of World War II

© Copyright 2024 - All rights reserved.

The content contained within this book may not be reproduced, duplicated, or transmitted without direct written permission from the author or the publisher.

Under no circumstances will any blame or legal responsibility be held against the publisher, or author, for any damages, reparation, or monetary loss due to the information contained within this book, either directly or indirectly.

Legal Notice:

This book is copyright protected. It is only for personal use. You cannot amend, distribute, sell, use, quote, or paraphrase any part, or the content within this book, without the consent of the author or publisher.

Disclaimer Notice:

Please note the information contained within this document is for educational and entertainment purposes only. All effort has been executed to present accurate, up-to-date, reliable, and complete information. No warranties of any kind are declared or implied. Readers acknowledge that the author is not engaging in the rendering of legal, financial, medical, or professional advice. The content within this book has been derived from various sources. Please consult a licensed professional before attempting any techniques outlined in this book.

By reading this document, the reader agrees that under no circumstances is the author responsible for any losses, direct or indirect, that are incurred as a result of the use of the information contained within this document, including, but not limited to, errors, omissions, or inaccuracies.

Free Bonus from Captivating History (Available for a Limited time)

Hi History Lovers!

Now you have a chance to join our exclusive history list so you can get your first history ebook for free as well as discounts and a potential to get more history books for free!

Simply visit the link below to join.

Or, Scan the QR code!

captivatinghistory.com/ebook

Also, make sure to follow us on Facebook, X, and YouTube by searching for Captivating History.

Table of Contents

INTRODUCTION: THE BEGINNING OF A MYSTERY 1
CHAPTER 1 - THE CRASH AT CÁDIZ 3
CHAPTER 2 - THE MAN WHO BECAME MINCEMEAT 7
CHAPTER 3 - THE DEAD MAN GOES FOR A SPIN................................11
CHAPTER 4 - THE FISHERMAN AND THE BODY 16
CHAPTER 5 - TRICKING THE TRICKSTERS..23
CHAPTER 6 - OPERATION MINCEMEAT HEATS UP 27
CHAPTER 7 - POWERFUL CONVICTIONS AT WORK 32
CHAPTER 8 - OPERATION MINCEMEAT: A STUNNING SUCCESS...........36
CONCLUSION: FALLING HOOK, LINE, AND SINKER...............................40
HERE'S ANOTHER BOOK BY CAPTIVATING HISTORY THAT YOU MIGHT LIKE 43
FREE BONUS FROM CAPTIVATING HISTORY (AVAILABLE FOR A LIMITED TIME) 44
FURTHER READING AND REFERENCE...45
IMAGE SOURCES 46

Introduction: The Beginning of a Mystery

Just picture it. The legendary Spanish harbor of Cádiz was being beaten and battered by ferocious gale-force winds and waves a mile high. These were the weather conditions on the fateful day of September 26th, 1942, the day a plane laden with Britain and its allies' best-laid plans came crashing down into the raging seas below.

Besides the terrible weather, this was a day to be remembered because it was the start of one of the most incredible schemes in human history. It was the start of a counterintelligence masterstroke dubbed "Operation Mincemeat."

At this point in the war, Spain was neutral. Francisco Franco's fascists had prevailed in the Spanish Civil War, but the pragmatic Franco, although himself a fascist, was not willing to pick sides in World War Two. As such, Spain had the odd and dubious honor of having the only fascist leader of World War II to survive and continue ruling well after the war came to a close.

Franco and his followers were determined to stay neutral, so whatever nation the plane belonged to, it was not considered a combatant at the time. The plane was simply more collateral damage of the war that had otherwise surrounded Spanish shores. The war was just like the winds that battered Cádiz, an external disturbance over which the Spaniards had no control and no interest in being any further part of.

However, when the corpses of this particular crash washed up on shore that day, it would be learned that they carried high-level military intelligence with them. This intelligence spelled out a major planned offensive against the Axis powers of Germany, Italy, and Japan.

Spain might have been neutral at the time, but it was still deeply connected to like-minded fascists in Italy and Germany. So, how would all of this play out? Would the Spanish just keep the information to themselves, or would they pass it on to their like-minded colleagues?

Chapter 1 – The Crash at Cádiz

"I have found a good man prepared to stick a limpet bomb on one of the larger German ships from a fishing boat, on a dark night with rain."

-Alan Hillgarth[i]

The dead body that washed up at Cádiz had a name: James Hadden Turner. He was a paymaster-lieutenant for the British Royal Navy and served as a courier. A briefcase had been chained to him. Its contents held important plans for an impending Allied invasion of French North Africa called Operation Torch, which was scheduled for November 4th, 1942.[ii]

This was an incredibly complicated operation, both logistically and politically. It was complicated on a political level because of the state of France. During the initial part of World War II in 1939, France was an ally of Britain. Britain and France declared war on Germany after Adolf Hitler ordered the invasion of Poland that year.

However, in the summer of 1940, the Germans shocked the world by defeating France. With the French capital occupied by German troops, the French were forced to sign an armistice with the Germans that had them not only cede northern France to the Nazis but also transformed

---

[i] Macintyre, Ben. *Operation Mincemeat: How a Dead Man and a Bizarre Plan Fooled the Nazis and Assured an Allied Victory.* 2010. Pg. 629.

[ii] Macintyre, Ben. *Operation Mincemeat: How a Dead Man and a Bizarre Plan Fooled the Nazis and Assured an Allied Victory.* Pg. 61.

southern France into a Nazi-friendly puppet state based out of the southern French city of Vichy.

Vichy France had been reduced to a rump state of its former self, but it still had wide-ranging colonies in Africa and Southeast Asia. France also had a huge naval fleet. The British made short work of a large portion of this fleet by taking the controversial step of launching an unprovoked attack against the French fleet while it was parked at Mers el-Kebir in French Algeria. This attack not only wiped out the fleet but also took the lives of around 1,300 French sailors.

If the British were worried that the French were no longer their friends, this incident certainly did not help matters much. Even if some French could logically conclude that it was wise for the British to destroy the craft lest they fall into German hands, the loss of some 1,300 people in one terrible, treacherous blow would be a hard pill for anyone to swallow.

Even so, by the time the United States was pulled into the war after being bombed by Japan in December of 1941, the British held out hope that British and US forces could make a joint landing in French Africa. Instead of fighting the French, it was hoped that they could convince the French to join them. As such, orders were given not to immediately engage the French forces and to only fight upon being fired upon.

This was the delicate political and logistical situation that the Allies faced in planning a joint landing in French North Africa in 1942. These were plans that they obviously wished to keep secret from the Germans and the other Axis powers. As such, fears that the war plans found on the downed airman at Cádiz might be intercepted by the Axis were very great indeed.

The letter the dead courier had on his person included the exact location and date of this offensive, as well as other pertinent information. If such data fell into the hands of the enemy, it would have been disastrous for the Allied war effort. Even more troubling was the fact that Cádiz, the locale where the body first washed up, was a known hub of German espionage.[1]

---

[1] Macintyre, Ben. *Operation Mincemeat: How a Dead Man and a Bizarre Plan Fooled the Nazis and Assured an Allied Victory.* Pg. 63.

This worried the supreme Allied commander, US General Dwight D. Eisenhower, to no end.[i] The Spanish authorities who had custody of the dead airman's body insisted that the deceased paymaster-lieutenant, as well as the personal belongings found on his corpse, were not trifled with and were still perfectly intact. Well, at least that is what they told the British.

The British wanted to trust the Spaniards, but they also needed to verify that what they said was true. As such, they sent over a team of specialists to examine the corpse and its personal artifacts themselves. This led to some intriguing discoveries. It was found that although the letter's seals had been opened, it was determined that they had not been opened by human hands. Instead, it was thought that seawater had broken the seals when the body had been submerged.

Another sign that the letter had not been messed with by those who found the body was due to the fact that sand was lodged in the coat pocket with the letter. It likely had not been messed with unless someone had been quick-thinking enough to remove a letter full of sand, read it, and then pack sand back in with it.[ii]

But even though this particular dead airman was not targeted, that did not mean that the other victims of the crash were not. Another passenger whose body later washed up on Spanish shores was a French intelligence officer by the name of Louis Daniélou, whom, it would be learned, had been obtained by German intelligence agents.

Daniélou had several documents taken from his person, including a notebook that outlined a vague summary of operational plans in North Africa. The intel he carried was not as significant as what Turner had on his person, but it was still a matter of concern. The fact that the Germans had gathered this bit of intelligence after the crash at Cádiz was realized when British operatives intercepted and decoded German chatter over the radio that indicated as much.

It was later learned that it was actually an Italian operative working in Spain who first received the data and then relayed it to the Germans. As it turned out, the Germans placed a low priority on this intel because

---

[i] Macintyre, Ben. *Operation Mincemeat: How a Dead Man and a Bizarre Plan Fooled the Nazis and Assured an Allied Victory.* Pg. 63.

[ii] Macintyre, Ben. *Operation Mincemeat: How a Dead Man and a Bizarre Plan Fooled the Nazis and Assured an Allied Victory.* Pg. 67.

The first task for British operatives was to find a dead body. Not only did they have to find a dead body, they also had to find one that no one would miss. They needed a man who had no ties. The British didn't need close family or friends inquiring as to what had happened to the remains.

The coroner, Bentley Purchase, was contacted with these strange requests, and it was learned that plenty of "unknowns" came into his custody on a regular basis. These unfortunate souls were drifters whose identity was not known, so any possible links to the world were just as murky. These were the kind of men who supposedly would not be missed. They were just the kind of unfortunate souls that British intelligence needed to pull off their ghoulish plot.

In the meantime, the Allies were debating on whether to launch their next major offensive against the Axis in Italian-controlled Sicily or German-occupied Greece. Just as the Allied powers had decided to make Sicily their next target, the coroner came across a dead body that suited the intelligence operatives' needs perfectly.

A Welsh drifter had been found dead in a rat-infested warehouse. He apparently had eaten a piece of bread laced with rat poisoning. It was a sad end to a sad life, but it opened a door of possibilities for the British, especially considering the cause of death.

For those who are unaware, rat poisoning causes the lungs to flood with fluid, suffocating the victim. As such, this man could appear to have died by drowning, making him the perfect candidate to be dumped on a beach with "top-secret" documents.

Since the Allied powers had decided to invade Sicily, intelligence operatives ramped up a deception plan to trick the Axis into thinking that Greece was the actual target. They began to cook up fake documents that could be put on the body of their dead accomplice, who would become known as "the man who never was."

But contrary to such appellations, he was indeed a real person, and he had a real (albeit sad) life. His name at birth was Glyndwr Michael, and he was born on January 4th, 1909. He was the son of a coal miner named Thomas John Michael and his wife Sarah Ann Chadwick.

This Welsh family apparently had a tough go of things. Mining is a rough way to make a living, and miners back in those days worked much harder and under much bleaker conditions for much less pay. Michael's primary duty was to haul loads of coal up dark and treacherous mine shafts, day in and day out. The pay was often not even enough for the family to pay their rent, which led to them having a semi-transient existence, constantly moving from one place to another. Besides the struggle to keep a roof over their heads, it was also an ongoing battle to put food on the table.

Matters became worse when Thomas Michael fell ill. He finally succumbed to his many years of working in the coal mine and was coughing up blood. By the time he was fifty-one years old, his condition had deteriorated to the point where he could no longer work. The family became entirely dependent on charity. Thomas Michael eventually developed pneumonia and passed away on March 31st, 1925.

This made sixteen-year-old Glyndwr Michael not only poor but also without a father. He had no direction in life and no resources to speak of whatsoever. He was at rock bottom, and the odds seemed to be against him. How could he ever climb up out of the disastrous circumstances that he had been born into? Records indicate that he was able to obtain some part-time work as a laborer and even a gardener, but times were tough in postwar Britain, and the job market was competitive for what few low-level jobs were available.

Glyndwr Michael's two sisters were a bit luckier because they were able to marry coal miners who were at least marginally successful at their trade and could provide for a family. Glyndwr, however, continued to struggle. After his mother perished on January 15th, 1940, he seemed to fall through the cracks entirely.

He ended up becoming a drifter. He made his way to London, where he lived mostly on the streets. There is a record that states he tried to find shelter at a lodging house in late 1942, likely so he could withstand the worst of winter. However, much of the time, he was either on the streets or squatting in abandoned buildings. It was in one of these abandoned buildings that Glyndwr was discovered on January 26th, 1943, dying from a case of poisoning.

It would later be found that he had ingested rat poisoning. Whether he did so on purpose or by accident is not entirely clear. It could have been that he was simply hungry, and living by the old saying "beggars can't be choosers," he ate some bread that had been left out. The only trouble was that the bread had been left out for rats and was laced with rat poison.

Then again, considering the sad mental state that Glyndwr was in, he could have known or even guessed that the bread contained rat poison and chose to eat it as a way to end his own life. Whatever the case may be, he perished shortly after he was found in that warehouse.

It must be noted that Glyndwr did survive long enough to be taken to the hospital, and it is said that he had one final moment of clarity before he passed. During this brief moment, Glyndwr Michael apparently told the nurses who cared for him his name and a few other details about how he had ended up in the state that he was in.

However, the damage to Glyndwr's organs had already been done, and he died on January 28th, 1943. He was thirty-four years old. The tragedy of his passing would soon turn into a great opportunity for the planners of Operation Mincemeat.

Chapter 3 – The Dead Man Goes for a Spin

"I was frightfully willing to help, always. I ran everywhere. I was so keen to please."

-Jean Leslie[i]

Shortly after the British coroner, Bentley Purchase, who was working in tandem with British intelligence, came across the newly deceased corpse of Glyndwr Michael, Operation Mincemeat began in earnest. Upon learning of Glyndwr's demise, Purchase dutifully alerted his contacts in British intelligence that he just might have what they had been looking for.

In Britain, the coroner works directly for the government and is involved in the investigation of how deaths occur.[ii] Although a cursory examination was conducted to understand the cause of death, no actual autopsy was carried out. This was due to the obvious need to keep the body as well preserved as possible. Any obvious cutting into the corpse would have alerted the very enemy agents that the Allies hoped to dupe. Such obvious tampering would have alerted them that the corpse, as well as the corresponding documents it carried, were entirely bogus.

---

[i] Macintyre, Ben. *Operation Mincemeat: How a Dead Man and a Bizarre Plan Fooled the Nazis and Assured an Allied Victory.* Pg. 301.

[ii] Macintyre, Ben. *Operation Mincemeat: How a Dead Man and a Bizarre Plan Fooled the Nazis and Assured an Allied Victory.* Pg. 37.

Time was of the essence, though, because the corpse had already begun to decay. The body could not be frozen, as was typically the case in the morgue, out of fear that liquid inside the corpse would expand and damage the body, rendering it suspicious to anyone who might later find it. It was determined that the corpse needed to be gotten rid of as soon as possible in order to successfully pull off this counterintelligence operation.

Initially, the operation had been referred to as Trojan Horse, but due to the necessity of obscuring the operation's purpose lest any chatter be picked up about it, the name was changed to the much vaguer yet frighteningly fitting name Operation Mincemeat.

Even though the operation was distastefully named, at least the dead man was given a respectable name. For this particular mission, British operatives named the dead man-turned-counterintelligence prop Major William Martin. The name Martin was chosen because it was such a common one.

Once the name was established, "Martin" was given corresponding fake identification documents to match. This created problems since it meant that he needed to have an ID badge. As far as anyone knew, Glyndwr Michael had no ID photos on file. It was deemed not to be smart to bother family members for a photo if such a photo even existed.

At first, intelligence operatives tried to pose the dead man to make him look somewhat alive for a proper photograph. This soon proved to be an impossible task since there was no way the cadaver's sunken eyes could be made to gleam with any spark of life.

It was quickly realized that there was no way that his dead body could be manipulated in a believable manner to make him appear as if he were anything other than dead. As such, it was realized that a stand-in would be needed. Fortunately for the intelligence operatives handling this mission, Glyndwr had rather average features. He had a face that could be easily lost in a crowd. It was just a matter of locating someone who had a vague resemblance to him.[1]

---

[1] Macintyre, Ben. *Operation Mincemeat: How a Dead Man and a Bizarre Plan Fooled the Nazis and Assured an Allied Victory.* Pg. 288.

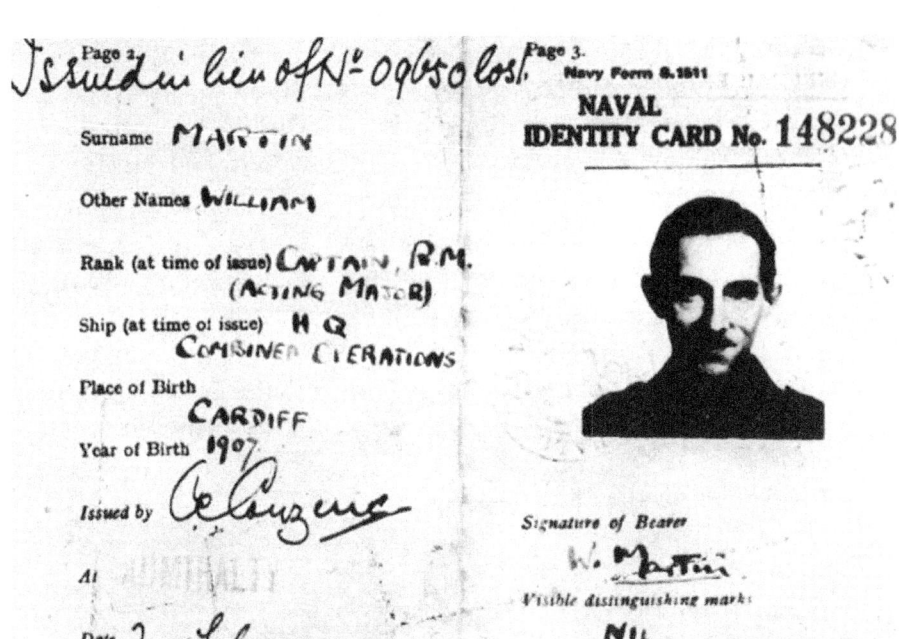

The ID card that British intelligence created.[1]

According to former intelligence agent Ewen Montagu, several hours were spent staring at men who came in and out of the office as they tried to find a match. They eventually settled for an MI5 captain by the name of Ronnie Reed, who put on the uniform of a royal marine and smiled for the camera. His face ended up on the ID card placed with the corpse.

Montagu played a crucial role in setting all of this up, and he became quite imaginative during the process. Thanks to his efforts, the fictional character established for the cadaver—Major William Martin—was given a backstory. Rather than being an impoverished pauper, airman William Martin was the son of a wealthy family from Wales. To further sweeten the pot, fabricated letters from his dear old dad were placed upon the corpse.

Identity discs with the name Major W. Martin engraved upon them were also placed on the body. These were small metal discs engraved with personal identity markers, such as the name of the individual who wore them, their rank, their service number, and the unit they belonged to. Military personnel wore these identity discs so they could be easily identified in case they were found incapacitated or deceased. Identity discs are more commonly known as dog tags in the United States.

Several other odds and ends, such as a receipt from dry cleaning, a used bus ticket, and a wad of cash, were placed on the corpse to give it a more realistic touch. The intelligence operatives behind this ruse figured that if the money suddenly vanished after the body had appeared, it would indicate that the corpse had been given a rather thorough inspection by whoever found it.

One of the more interesting final touches was depositing a photo of an attractive young lady, who was made out to be the dead man's fiancé—a woman dubbed "Pam." But in reality, this lady was a twenty-year-old secretary, Jean Leslie, for the intelligence office back in London. Some fabricated fictional love letters were included for good measure. These love letters were written by Jean's supervisor in the office, a stern, no-nonsense woman by the name of Hester Leggett.

The photograph of the fake "Pam." [2]

Around the office, Hester Leggett was nicknamed "The Spin" in reference to her being an old "spinster" who had never married.[1] It was with some irony that these gushing love letters were written by a lady whom her coworkers had so callously written off as an old spinster.

---

[1] Macintyre, Ben. *Operation Mincemeat: How a Dead Man and a Bizarre Plan Fooled the Nazis and Assured an Allied Victory.* Pg. 110.

Once the corpse was dressed up with all of the proper trappings of a soldier in uniform, Major W. Martin was loaded onto a submarine called HMS *Seraph*, which was under the authority of Lieutenant Bill Jewell.

Chapter 4 – The Fisherman and the Body

"You can't get bodies just for the asking, you know. I should think bodies are the only commodities not in short supply at the moment [but] even with bodies all over the place, each one has to be accounted for."

-The coroner, Bentley Purchase[1]

At the Casablanca Conference in January 1943, Allied war planners decided to invade Sicily rather than launch an invasion of Greece and the Balkans, even though a successful invasion of Greece would have enabled the Allies to potentially box in the Germans on the Eastern Front. British and American forces would be on one side, and the Soviet Russians would be on the other. This plan was quickly passed up when it was determined that German defenses in this region, as well as their support from their Balkan allies, were too formidable. Rather than risk getting bogged down in the Balkans, the Allies could use Sicily as a stepping stone into Europe's so-called "soft underbelly."

Although Sicily had been decided as the target, British military intelligence wanted the Germans to keep thinking that Greece was about to be invaded. As such, several fake documents indicating an invasion of Greece were stashed on the dead body of a recently deceased Welsh vagrant, Glyndwr Michael.

---

[1] Macintyre, Ben. *Operation Mincemeat: How a Dead Man and a Bizarre Plan Fooled the Nazis and Assured an Allied Victory.* Pg. 181.

In April 1943, the corpse was sent on a collision course with the Spanish port city of Huelva. Although the dead man's backstory called for him to be in the employ of the Royal Air Force, the corpse was placed inside a hermetically sealed container that was then placed on board a submarine, the HMS *Seraph*.

The officers of HMS Seraph.[3]

Lieutenant Bill Jewell, the captain of the ship, was thirty years old at the time and already a well-known component of British naval operations. He had served in fierce battles against enemy craft from the Mediterranean Sea to the Atlantic Ocean. He had survived several brushes with death, narrowly avoiding torpedoes and machine gun fire. He also nearly perished when his crippled sub was forced to hide at the bottom of the sea for several hours, nearly running out of oxygen in the process. However, the mission he carried out that April was not so much a brush with death as it was a conveyance of death.

Interestingly, as an indication of just how compartmentalized British military intelligence was, Lieutenant Jewell had no idea who the dead man was. He did not even know the exact purpose of the operation. All he knew was that it was of great importance and had to be kept secret.[i] Jewell told his rank-and-file crewmen that the canister they carried was part of a top-secret meteorological experiment that was to be conducted in Spanish waters.

It is hard to tell why weather research, meteorological equipment, weather balloons, and the like are so often used as cover stories for top-secret missions. Such things have been used in the past to cover up instances of snooping on nuclear powers, downed U-2 flights, and other forms of espionage.

The main reason for the secrecy was to keep the details of their mission as quiet as possible and avoid any potential leakage of data that could compromise the mission's main objective. Another reason to keep the majority of the crew in the dark was for their own sense of comfort. Jewell later remarked about how sailors were known to be a bit on the superstitious side, and if they knew they had been carting around a corpse, they might have had some grave (no pun intended) misgivings about the whole thing.

Upon arriving near the port of Huelva, this precious, top-secret cargo that Lieutenant Jewell had dutifully ferried was removed from the submarine. Up until this point, the corpse had been concealed inside a sealed capsule. This particular containment unit was the brainchild of Charles Fraser-Smith, a genius inventor of several innovations for Britain's secret service.[ii]

The capsule was made of steel and was six and a half feet long and roughly two feet in diameter. The steel hull of the capsule consisted of a so-called "double skin," which allowed for spacing between the two steel layers, where asbestos wool was packed for extra insulation. The interior of the capsule had been packed with dry ice, and oxygen had been carefully limited so as to provide the best preservation possible for the corpse.

Before the body was dropped into the water, a few select crew members (high-ranking officers who obviously were in the know about the true contents of the capsule) attended to the corpse, taking the body

---

[i] Macintyre, Ben. *Operation Mincemeat: How a Dead Man and a Bizarre Plan Fooled the Nazis and Assured an Allied Victory.* Pg. 555.

[ii] Macintyre, Ben. *Operation Mincemeat: How a Dead Man and a Bizarre Plan Fooled the Nazis and Assured an Allied Victory.* Pg. 447.

out of the capsule and placing it in the water. The body was held aloft by an inflated life jacket. A dinghy was also placed nearby for good measure.[1]

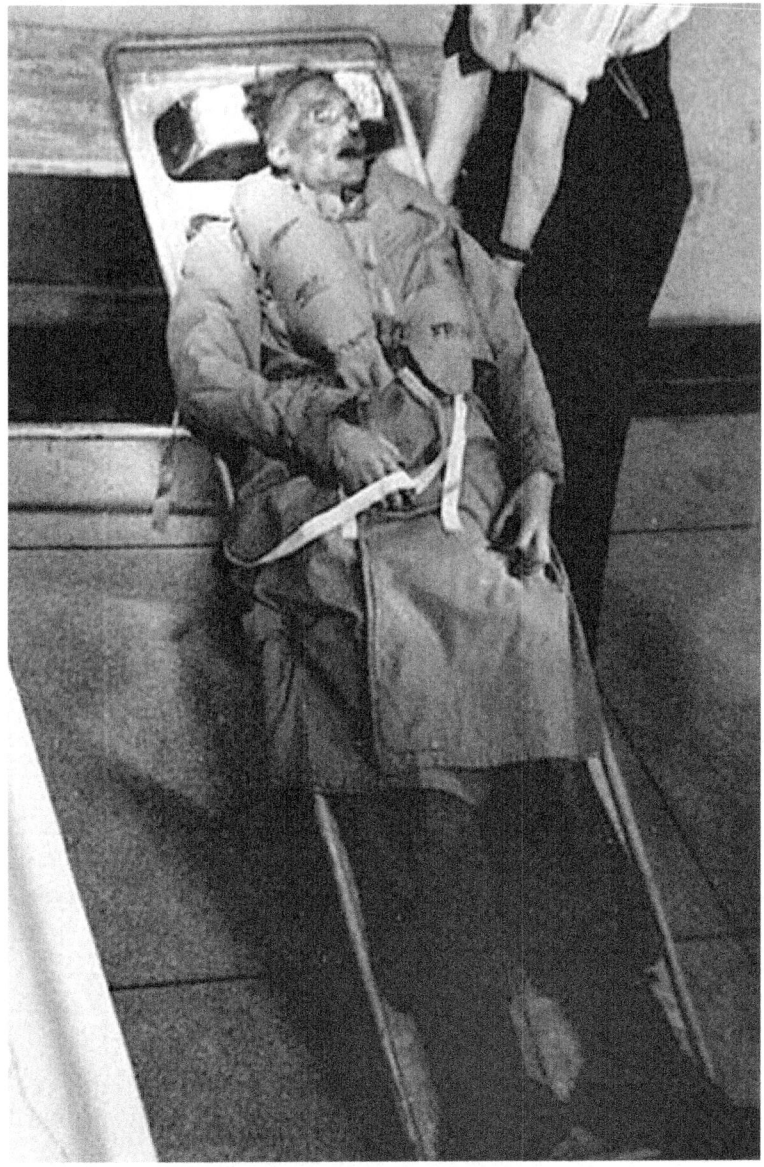

The body of Glyndwr Michael.[4]

---

[1] Macintyre, Ben. *Operation Mincemeat: How a Dead Man and a Bizarre Plan Fooled the Nazis and Assured an Allied Victory.* Pg. 563.

This set the scene of a dead airman who had fallen out of a dinghy. The dead body and the documents placed on its person were then sent floating in the direction of the port of Huelva, Spain.

What happened to the capsule was another story. The initial plan called for the capsule to be disposed of. However, this was easier said than done. The capsule was designed to be buoyant and proved incredibly hard to sink. The crew shot it to pieces with their guns, but it still floated to the surface. Even more alarming, it seemed ready to tag right along with the corpse in the dinghy all the way to Huelva.

Out of desperation, Jewell and his officers opted to plant plastic explosives on the capsule. They then lit the fuse and backed away before the capsule was blown to bits.

Sinking the capsule by means of an explosion presented a grave risk since it drew attention to their operation. Fishing craft had already been spotted in the distance, and they were likely to have taken notice. Even so, Jewell gambled that once the dead body washed up, those who found him would later correlate the loud explosion with the body, assuming that it was part of what had brought the supposed dead airman down. Fortunately, for the sake of their mission, this seems to have been the case. The explosion of the capsule did not blow their cover.

Interestingly, Captain Jewell did not reveal this aspect of the mission until several decades later. It was not until 1991 that an elderly Jewell finally confessed to blowing up the capsule. Previously, he had only reported that he and his officers shot holes in the capsule.

The first person to come into contact with this intelligence payload was a local Spanish fisherman by the name of José Antonio Rey María. Twenty-three-year-old José was not working for any intelligence outfit. He was just a simple fisherman seeking to catch enough fish to earn him a livable wage. He was actually hunting for sardines, the tiny little specialty fish of the Mediterranean, which he hoped would fetch him a good price at the fish market.

José was a skilled fisherman and was already well esteemed as a man who could bring in a good catch. His eyes were especially gifted at noticing underwater schools of fish from far away. His keen vision could easily pick out the swarms of sardines moving from one place to another underneath the surface of the water. But little did anyone know the highly unusual find he would haul in on April 30th, 1943.

On that particular day, visibility was fairly bad due to stormy weather the day before. Even so, later that morning, José was able to notice a definite shape of some sort moving just near the surface. Since sardines normally travel much deeper, he initially was not sure what he was seeing, but he knew it likely did not have anything to do with the fish that he was looking for.

Even so, he sent his small boat sailing toward the dark, submerged shape to see what he could figure out. As he got closer, something bright and yellow caught his eye. He soon realized that he was looking at a submerged life jacket. He soon realized that this life jacket was attached to what looked like a person.

José looked closely at the figure and could see that they were decked out in a uniform of some sort, indicating that they were likely military personnel. Spain was neutral, but in the midst of war, military men were a common enough site.

As José leaned over the side of his boat to get a better look, he could see that this man had clearly seen better days. His face was burned, and his nose was almost completely rotted off. The smell of death was quite unmistakable.

This was a bit much for José to handle by himself, so he quickly waved other nearby fishermen over for assistance. These men approached, but after taking a look at the corpse, they made it clear that they wanted nothing to do with it. With great reluctance, José ended up grabbing the man by his uniform and hauling him into his own boat all by himself.

He managed to bring the body to shore, where a fisherman friend of his helped him drag the corpse to more stable ground on the beach. As they dragged the man, a black briefcase was dragged right along with the body. The briefcase was curiously attached to the corpse by way of a chain. Whatever it was, it was obviously important.

The two men soon reached the shade of a nearby pine tree, where they decided to temporarily stop to rest. Local kids stopped to stare at the strange sight. The dead man must have been tall and imposing during his life. The corpse stretched out some six feet. He wore a khaki uniform complete with combat boots and a long trench coat. He also had a silver cross hanging from his throat, tipping off people that the man was a Christian.

Shortly after, the Spanish military was alerted to what was happening, and a military officer came to investigate. The officer was quick to post guards around the dead body in order to ensure that no one stole anything from the deceased man's person. They stood guard while a donkey was dispatched for transportation. It might not have been the most effective means of transport, but this donkey-turned-hearse would have to do.

The plan was to have the donkey take the body to nearby Punta Umbria, where it could then be loaded onto a boat and carried across the waters to the port city of Huelva.

As for the identity of the downed airman? A quick check of his wallet indicated that he was Major William Martin. The name itself might not have rang any bells among the Spanish authorities, but they knew that someone, somewhere (whether they be British or German) would be interested in the find.

The man who kickstarted this whole chain of events, José Antonio Rey María, was already back to his fishing, blissfully unaware of the commotion that was about to ensue.

Chapter 5 – Tricking the Tricksters

"It seemed that the listening in was done by an Abwehr member, but it might have been done by a Spanish telephone operator. Abwehr wireless traffic made it clear that a senior Spanish official had been 'squared' to allow the tapping. Only by naval ciphers can really safe messages be sent."

-Alan Hillgarth[i]

Even though Spain was officially neutral during World War II, the Spanish coasts were constantly being littered with collateral damage from the war. Planes crashed, bodies turned up, and other miscellaneous items of either little or great importance found their way onto the shores of Spain.

The body that was found on April 30th, 1943, was transported to Huelva by Spanish troops. The Spanish then engaged in a bit of theater, which involved the Spaniards and a British operative on the ground, Vice Consul Francis Haselden, who was part of the British foreign services department in Spain.

The Spaniards, for their part, knew they needed to appear to be following official protocol in the eyes of the British. This resulted in a

---

[i] Macintyre, Ben. *Operation Mincemeat: How a Dead Man and a Bizarre Plan Fooled the Nazis and Assured an Allied Victory.* Pg. 619.

series of back-and-forth diplomatic cables staged for show, which reported the findings. The cables were encrypted, but the Spanish officials likely knew—as the British knew—that these encrypted messages were easily understood by the Germans, who had cracked the code long ago. The British knew that the Germans eavesdropped on this channel.

Vice Consul Francis Haselden played it up as the British point of contact. The Spaniards wished to convey both their neutrality and a general lack of interest in the body and the documents it carried. After first being presented with the corpse and the documents by Pascual del Pobil, a Spanish contact he knew well, Haselden declined to take custody of the body. He realized that taking hold of the body would defeat the whole purpose of the ruse, so he insisted on going through the typical routine of alerting his superior officers and having the body undergo an autopsy.

The autopsy was a rather simple affair. It was conducted by a civilian forensic pathologist whose name was Dr. Eduardo Fernández del Torno. The good doctor apparently did not probe too deeply and very quickly assumed that the unfortunate downed airman had drowned. To the delight of Haselden, the findings were quick and concise, and the case was closed without any further inquiries being made.[i]

It was declared that the man had fallen into the ocean, had perished from asphyxia due to being submerged in the waters, and had likely perished some eight to ten days prior to his body being found.[ii] A more detailed autopsy that actually examined the lungs, liver, and kidney might have identified the traces of phosphorous poison in the body.

But this cursory examination done by Dr. Eduardo Fernández del Torno was not able to determine such things. Even so, Dr. Torno noted certain peculiarities that did not seem to sit well with the theory that the man had drowned at sea. For one thing, he knew from experience that someone who had been in the water for over a week should have soggy, nearly unrecognizable clothing. Yet, this man's fresh and crisp uniform seemed as if it had taken a spin in the washer because after drying out, the clothes were none the worse for wear. It just did not look like the

---

[i] Macintyre, Ben. *Operation Mincemeat: How a Dead Man and a Bizarre Plan Fooled the Nazis and Assured an Allied Victory.* Pg. 469.

[ii] Macintyre, Ben. *Operation Mincemeat: How a Dead Man and a Bizarre Plan Fooled the Nazis and Assured an Allied Victory.* Pg. 473.

uniform of a man who had been waterlogged for over a week.

Perhaps even more problematic was that the body, although beaten up and obviously having suffered trauma, did not look like it had been feasted upon by denizens of the sea. Usually, when someone has been in the water for any length of time, the body will show signs of having been bit by fish or attacked by crabs or other sea creatures. However, these marks were not on the victim.[i]

Francis Haselden and the British officials paid close attention as the body and the documents it carried went through the standard protocol. As information was fed through official Spanish channels of government, it was hoped that the Germans would get wind of what was happening. And sure enough, they did.

The German agents soon began to apply pressure on the Spaniards to reveal the contents of the retrieved documents. The Spaniards did not want to ruffle any feathers on either side, so they secretly complied in a way (at least so they thought) that would not rock the boat with the British.

The Spanish carefully removed documents and had them photographed before putting them back in place, doing their best to make sure that nothing looked outwardly disturbed. They passed these photos to the Germans as they readied the corpse and the original contents it carried to be sent back to the British.

The designated British naval operative on the ground, Francis Haselden, played a very interesting role in all of this. He was careful to be consistent with his requests to have the body and its documents returned intact while not being too overly zealous about it. The last thing the British wanted was for Haselden to be so convincing about how imperative it was to get the documents back that British pressure trumped German pressure. Such an overreach might have actually resulted in the Spaniards sending the body and its fake documents back to Britain quickly without allowing the deceptive information to fall into German hands.

That, of course, would have defeated the whole purpose of Operation Mincemeat. The purpose was for the Germans to believe they had gotten one over on the British and had uncovered Britain's war plans.

---

[i] Macintyre, Ben. *Operation Mincemeat: How a Dead Man and a Bizarre Plan Fooled the Nazis and Assured an Allied Victory.* Pg. 475.

This was the façade that needed to be pushed in order for the Germans to bolster their defenses in Greece and the Balkans in preparation for an Allied invasion that would not come.

Chapter 6 – Operation Mincemeat Heats Up

"We felt that we knew him just as one knows one's best friend. We had come to feel that we had known Bill Martin from his earliest childhood, [knowing] his every thought and his probable reaction to any event that might occur in his life."

-Ewen Montagu[i]

Major William Martin was buried with full military honors at a cemetery in Huelva, Spain. It was not unusual in those days to bury dead soldiers where they died rather than go through all the trouble of repatriating them back home. And that is what happened to Glyndwr Michael, also known as Major William Martin, who was laid to rest at Nuestra Senora cemetery on May 2nd, 1943.

Of course, he wasn't really a soldier at all—at least not in the traditional sense. Glyndwr Michael had never served in the military a day in his life. He was dead, not from an act of valor but one of desperation. Even so, his posthumous contributions to the war effort had tremendous implications for the war.

On May 5th, senior Spanish naval officer Captain Francisco Elvira Álvarez informed British Vice Consul Haselden that the body's

---

[i] Macintyre, Ben. *Operation Mincemeat: How a Dead Man and a Bizarre Plan Fooled the Nazis and Assured an Allied Victory.* Pg. 370-371.

belongings were being sent up the chain command all the way to his own superior officer stationed in San Fernando. In San Fernando, arrangements were made for the body and its personal effects to be sent to the Ministry of Marine in Madrid. At the same time, however, he also tipped off his German point of contact, Adolf Clauss.

The Spanish authorities dutifully returned the briefcase to the British but not before its contents were photographed by Spaniards loyal to Germany. Photos were taken of the documents, which were extracted without opening their packages. The Spanish did this by twisting the documents out of the side of the envelopes they were in without breaking the seals that held them closed.

Once the water-logged papers had been removed, they were quickly dried by a special heat lamp, which allowed them to be better handled during their examination by Spain's German contacts. After the Germans were through with them, the dried-out documents were carefully soaked in salt water again before being carefully twisted back through the sides of the envelopes, still without breaking the seals. Since the seals were not broken, there was nothing to alert the people in Madrid that anything had been tampered with.

The British anticipated the tactics that were employed and had supposedly put a black eyelash in one of the envelopes to detect the faintest disruption. So, even though the seals were intact, this planted eyelash had fallen out during the struggle to extract the documents. There were other telltale signs of tampering, such as the fact that the papers that had been shoved back into the envelopes had been folded differently than the originals. Upon closer inspection, two specific sets of fold lines could clearly be seen.

After the important documents had been extracted, Spanish Lieutenant Colonel Pardo took them to the German embassy. However, he did not hand them over to the Germans to take ownership of them. The Germans were explicitly told they were allowed one hour to look over the paperwork. After that, the documents had to be returned.

The nature of Pardo's relationship with the Germans was not fully known until near the end of the war. In April of 1945, as the Nazis were on the brink of defeat, a group of British intel agents came across a treasure trove of secret German archives stashed at Tambach Castle in Coburg, Germany. Interestingly enough, these operatives were working on the direct orders of Ian Fleming, the man who later created the character of James Bond, upon whom he partially projected some of his own life experiences. This intel stash at Coburg revealed information about Pardo. He was just an average Spanish staff officer, but he had forged strong connections with the German military intelligence group, the Abwehr.[i]

It is perhaps a strange offer that the Spaniards gave the Germans, but it is perhaps even stranger that the Germans complied. The Germans were known to be rather ruthless after all, so what made them comply with the Spaniard's request to give all of the documents back unharmed and intact after an hour had passed?

Well, it seems that the Germans embraced pragmatism. The situation in Spain was very delicate and complicated. Spain was neutral, and there were both pro-German and pro-British factions in Spain at the time. The Germans very much wished to keep the delicate balance of neutral Spain intact, at least for the time being, and this meant the Germans were willing to play by the rules of the high-stakes game of subterfuge that the Spaniards were playing.

At any rate, the letters were handed over to the German Abwehr (Germany's military intelligence and counterintelligence) chief, Admiral Wilhelm Canaris, who immediately ordered one of his subordinates to have them photocopied. Once the photocopying was complete, the original documents were handed back to Lieutenant Colonel Pardo.[ii] The delicate task of removing the documents was then reversed, with the documents twisted around and placed back into their envelopes without breaking their seals or even creasing the paperwork inside.[iii]

The photocopies were sent to another member of the Abwehr, Karl-Erich Kuhlenthal, who brought the copied documents back to Germany.[iv] It seems that Karl-Erich Kuhlenthal, a man with a flair for the dramatic, embellished certain details in regard to how the documents

---

[i] Macintyre, Ben. *Operation Mincemeat: How a Dead Man and a Bizarre Plan Fooled the Nazis and Assured an Allied Victory.* Pg. 355.

[ii] Macintyre, Ben. *Operation Mincemeat: How a Dead Man and a Bizarre Plan Fooled the Nazis and Assured an Allied Victory.* Pg. 569.

[iii] Macintyre, Ben. *Operation Mincemeat: How a Dead Man and a Bizarre Plan Fooled the Nazis and Assured an Allied Victory.* Pg. 569.

[iv] Macintyre, Ben. *Operation Mincemeat: How a Dead Man and a Bizarre Plan Fooled the Nazis and Assured an Allied Victory.* Pg. 571.

were discovered and the circumstances of them being copied for German consumption. He made it seem as if he were there when the documents were removed from the envelopes, which he was not. He also claimed that the dead body had been found clutching the briefcase in its arms. This was also not true. After these supposed findings had been recorded, Kuhlenthal rushed off with the copied documents to speak with his taskmasters in Berlin.

The originals were ferreted over to the British embassy in Spain by Admiral Alfonso Arriago Adam, who was serving as the Spanish navy's chief of staff at the time. Admiral Alfonso arrived at the embassy with the documents on May 11th.[i] He handed the documents over to his British point of contact, Naval Attaché Alan Hillgarth.[ii]

Hillgarth was an experienced British hand in Spain and had already served as a vital link between the two sides during the Spanish Civil War. Hillgarth was involved in several high-level prisoner swaps between the two warring sides during Spain's civil unrest, earning him great trust on both sides.

Even though the Spanish Civil War had come to a close, Hillgarth was still an important player in Spain and had been promoted to the role of naval attaché in Madrid.[iii] As it pertains to Operation Mincemeat, Hillgarth was in on the whole thing from the start and knew that he had to put on a look of serious concern while not showing any undue suspicion that might alert anyone that the British knew that the documents had been tampered with.

Just a casual glance told him that items had been moved around, but Hillgarth continued his façade of disinterest. He had the items repackaged and readied to be sent off to Britain's intelligence department in London.

That same day, May 11th, the Germans were busy working on their first official assessment of the confiscated copies of the documents. These were signed off on by a German intelligence operative named

---

[i] Macintyre, Ben. *Operation Mincemeat: How a Dead Man and a Bizarre Plan Fooled the Nazis and Assured an Allied Victory.* Pg. 585.

[ii] Macintyre, Ben. *Operation Mincemeat: How a Dead Man and a Bizarre Plan Fooled the Nazis and Assured an Allied Victory.* Pg. 585.

[iii] Macintyre, Ben. *Operation Mincemeat: How a Dead Man and a Bizarre Plan Fooled the Nazis and Assured an Allied Victory.* Pg. 599.

Baron Alexis von Roenne.

The report had the somewhat bland yet appropriate title of "Discovery of the English Courier." British war and operation plans had been found on the dead body of what the Germans consistently referred to as "an English courier."[ii]

The report relayed what was then supposedly "discovered" in the copied documents in regard to a major amphibious assault supposedly planned by the British in the eastern Mediterranean. It was also learned that the name of the plan was Operation Husky.

As it turns out, the name of the operation was about the only factual thing the Germans learned.[iii] Although the next major offensive was codenamed Operation Husky, it was not going to take place in the eastern Mediterranean near Greece but rather in the western Mediterranean in an all-out invasion of the island of Sicily.

Now every time German operatives heard chatter of the impending Operation Husky, they would smugly bolster defenses in Greece and the Balkans, thinking they were getting one over on the wily British. They did this while seriously neglecting assets in Sicily, making the island vulnerable to an Allied offensive. This was, of course, exactly what British intelligence operatives had in mind.

---

[i] Macintyre, Ben. *Operation Mincemeat: How a Dead Man and a Bizarre Plan Fooled the Nazis and Assured an Allied Victory.* Pg. 599.

[ii] Macintyre, Ben. *Operation Mincemeat: How a Dead Man and a Bizarre Plan Fooled the Nazis and Assured an Allied Victory.* Pg. 601.

[iii] Macintyre, Ben. *Operation Mincemeat: How a Dead Man and a Bizarre Plan Fooled the Nazis and Assured an Allied Victory.* Pg. 602.

Chapter 7 – Powerful Convictions at Work

"Spain contained a large number of German agents and plenty of Spaniards in German pay. They had some ingenious ideas. We did our best to learn their plans, and to some extent succeeded. Madrid was full of spies. No one is watched all the time, but everyone is watched some of the time."

-Alan Hillgarth[i]

On May 14th, 1943, the official documents found with the supposed downed airman Major William Martin left Madrid by plane in a sealed carrier bag.[ii] On that very day, German Grand Admiral Karl Dönitz had an in-depth discussion with Hitler on the matter. The discussion revealed that Hitler was convinced that the British were aiming for Greece, at least in part because of the documents found on the airman's body.

In order to entertain this belief, Hitler had to overrule his good buddy Benito Mussolini. The Italian dictator Mussolini had been quite insistent that the invasion would most likely not be in Greece but on his own doorstep of Sicily. However, Hitler refused to believe Mussolini, as he

---

[i] Macintyre, Ben. *Operation Mincemeat: How a Dead Man and a Bizarre Plan Fooled the Nazis and Assured an Allied Victory.* Pg. 409.

[ii] Macintyre, Ben. *Operation Mincemeat: How a Dead Man and a Bizarre Plan Fooled the Nazis and Assured an Allied Victory.* Pg. 589.

continued to view the Balkans as the most likely place where the two forces would collide.

Putting his money where his mouth was, he acted on his hunch, sending several German divisions to Greece. Prior to the deception of Operation Mincemeat, Greece only boasted one division, yet there were suddenly eight.

Interestingly enough, as much as the Germans were convinced that an attack on Greece was imminent, they wanted the British to think that they thought nothing of the sort. In order to convince the Allied forces that the German high command was under the impression that Sicily was the target, they pretended to bolster Sicily while actually not making much of an effort to defend it at all. It was a duplicitous game afoot, as the Germans had been tricked and were doing their best to trick the British.

But no matter what the Germans wanted the British to believe, they were, in fact, duped by the dead body and the documents found with it, so much so that the aforementioned intelligence chief Baron von Roenne had basically concluded that the information found with the dead man was infallible and that there was no indication whatsoever that anything was planted on the corpse to deceive anyone.[i]

It was perhaps the nature of the find. If, for example, a briefcase just happened to wash up on the shores of Spain, this might have been viewed with more suspicion. But these documents had been accompanied by a dead airman. The British were known to respect their fallen soldiers. Would they really be disrespectful enough to use a dead body to plant fake documents?

This was likely something that the German analysts openly speculated about. It is said Hitler himself even posed this question at one point.[ii] But even so, it was quickly dismissed as a possibility. They likely figured it was inconceivable that the British would even do such a thing, so they stuck to the notion that the documents were legitimate.

---

[i] Macintyre, Ben. *Operation Mincemeat: How a Dead Man and a Bizarre Plan Fooled the Nazis and Assured an Allied Victory.* Pg. 609.

[ii] Macintyre, Ben. *Operation Mincemeat: How a Dead Man and a Bizarre Plan Fooled the Nazis and Assured an Allied Victory.* Pg. 639.

However, there is another theory about all of this, and this one involves willful self-sabotage on the part of some members of the German intelligence. This theory posits that German intelligence figures, such as Baron Alexis von Roenne, did suspect that the documents were fakes but led the German military into a trap out of a secret desire to undermine Nazi Germany. Considering how von Roenne's life ultimately ended, the likelihood of such things seems rather strong. Von Roenne was executed in 1944 by the Nazi regime after he was linked to the underground resistance led by Claus von Stauffenberg, which resulted in a failed plot to kill Hitler.

Claus von Stauffenberg was an interesting character. For much of his life, he was a loyal soldier to the German regime, but by 1944, when the war was going badly, he began to consider the terrible destruction that Hitler had unleashed. Stauffenberg decided to take a stand against Hitler. In retrospect, some have wondered if this stand was only due to the fact that the Germans were losing the war.

Either way, taking a stand was no small feat since, at this stage, almost all opposition to the Nazis' totalitarian rule had already been cowed into submission. Stauffenberg worked to undermine Hitler while still playing the part of a loyal Nazi stooge. It was only after the failure of the July plot that his treachery was uncovered.

In the aftermath, Clause von Stauffenberg and Baron Alexis von Roenne were denounced as traitors. Stauffenberg's hand in the plot was direct and clear, but Roenne's culpability was multifaceted and more subtle. There is no clear evidence he was directly involved, but there is evidence that he was aware the plot was about to take place through his own personal contacts. The fact that Roenne knew that Stauffenberg was actively orchestrating a plot to kill Hitler and did nothing about it was more than enough to have him branded a traitor.

Besides any connections to Stauffenberg and the July plot, it was learned that von Roenne had been quietly undermining German war plans for some time. To the chagrin of top Nazis, it was discovered Roenne had willfully accepted faulty information surrounding the D-Day invasion, allowing the Germans to be duped once again. Baron Alexis von Roenne kept trumpeting misinformation about a potential landing at Calais. The Allies, of course, landed in Normandy, France. Calais was just a bluff.

Roenne paid the price for his duplicity. He was killed by the Nazis in the most brutal of fashion. On October 11th, 1944, just as the walls were starting to close in on the Nazi regime, von Roenne was hung from a meat hook and left to die a slow and agonizing death.[i]

---

[i] Macintyre, Ben. *Operation Mincemeat: How a Dead Man and a Bizarre Plan Fooled the Nazis and Assured an Allied Victory*. Pg. 68.

Chapter 8 – Operation Mincemeat: A Stunning Success

"Intelligence, like food, soon gets stale, smelly, cold, soggy and indigestible, and when it has gone bad does more harm than good. If it ever gets into one of these revolting conditions, do not try to warm it up. Withdraw the offending morsel, and start again."

-John Godfrey, British naval intelligence[i]

The invasion of Sicily was a stunning success. The invasion was launched on July 25th, 1943. On that fateful day, the Allies found the Italian and German defenses of Sicily severely lacking. The defenses were not just neglected; they had been relegated as being altogether unimportant.

As a demonstration of just how convinced the Germans were that Sicily was not the real target of the Allies, even as the invasion itself was underway, instead of reinforcing Sicily, orders were given to send several fighter planes out of Sicily. These craft were relocated to Sardinia, where the German high command was convinced that the main invasion force would arrive before striking Greece and advancing into the Balkans.

There would be no Balkan invasion, though, and it would take several precious hours for the German authorities to admit they had made a big

---

[i] Macintyre, Ben. *Operation Mincemeat: How a Dead Man and a Bizarre Plan Fooled the Nazis and Assured an Allied Victory.* Pg. 212.

mistake. This allowed the Allies to basically steamroll right over Sicily, leading to a spectacular victory. Sicily fell into Allied hands on August 17th, 1943.

Initially, Allied war planners figured that the battle for Sicily would last a few months, but victory was achieved in just a fraction of that predicted timeframe. The Allies were able to gain air superiority over the island rather quickly (just think of all those fighter craft ordered away from Sicily). This was a great boon to the Allies, who had much to fear from the seasoned Luftwaffe.

If Sicily had been properly defended by both air power in the sky and air defenses on the ground, the outcome likely would have been much different. The American forces were still a bit raw and inexperienced, especially compared to the Luftwaffe. The American soldiers had fought some major battles in North Africa, but they were still a bit green as it pertained to launching a major amphibious invasion.

This invasion of Sicily was, in many ways, the dress rehearsal for the even more massive and complicated D-Day invasion. The fact that the Allies were able to conduct it with very little opposition gave them the perfect real-life practical experience they needed to learn how to conduct future invasions on a much larger scale. Many mistakes were made during the course of the operation, such as paratroopers being dropped in the wrong locations. These amateur mistakes would have turned into deadly mistakes if the defenses on Sicily had been more formidable.

Nevertheless, due to the lack of proper defense, an amphibious invasion was successfully carried out, resulting in the rapid advancement of an overland invasion force. The Allies had not just easily acquired an important strategic outpost in the Mediterranean, but the ease of their success had also thoroughly shocked the Italians. There were even calls for Italian Prime Minister Benito Mussolini to be ousted.

It is important to note that although Mussolini was a dictator of similar stripes as Hitler, Mussolini did not have Italy under his complete control, unlike his German counterpart. Benito was a dictator only at the pleasure of the Italian people and, more importantly, the king of Italy, Victor Emmanuel III.

As such, when it was clear that the war was going very badly for Italy, the Italians were able to find mechanisms to relieve themselves of Benito Mussolini. Ultimately, he was summoned by the king, who dismissed him from power. In his place, Italian General Pietro Badoglio was made the temporary sitting prime minister.

Hitler was infuriated by these developments since Benito Mussolini was one of the few men he actually considered to be a friend of his. But as long as the Italians promised to keep up the war effort against the Allies, he held his tongue.

Most Italians did not want to keep fighting the Allies, though. The king realized that popular sentiment was against the war, and he did not wish to continue the disastrous engagement any further. Even so, he knew full well that decoupling his nation from Germany would not be an easy task. He knew that as soon as the Germans got any hint that Italy was about to surrender, they would get the same treatment France had. The French had been bulldozed by the Germans and had a fascist puppet state foisted upon them. The Italians knew they would be in for the same treatment—or worse—if they suddenly declared themselves neutral, let alone switch sides.

As such, the king and the new prime minister kept up the façade of still being in the fight for fascism, even while Prime Minister Badoglio opened up a secret channel with the Allies to discuss Italy's surrender. Such discussions could not be kept secret forever. After an official surrender was announced over the radio by US General and Supreme Allied Commander Dwight D. Eisenhower, the Germans moved in.

The Germans sent their forces crashing through the Alps and took over northern Italy by force. The king and his court were forced to relocate. Hitler did not forget about his friend Mussolini, who had been imprisoned. He sent in German commandos, and in a daring raid that involved paratroopers, they managed to free the former dictator.

Mussolini was put in charge of a fascist puppet state in northern Italy. He knew that he was nothing more than a puppet at this point, and he also likely knew that his own days were numbered. The walls were definitely closing in on him, as well as what was left of Italy's fascist regime.

Although cleaving away at least half of the Italian Peninsula and establishing a beachhead against the Axis in southern Italy was certainly beneficial for the Allies, there were some unintended consequences. The sudden ousting of Mussolini (at least in the south) led to a resurgence in the popularity of the Italian Communist Party. Mussolini's followers, for all of their faults, had been keeping down the Partito Comunista Italiano (PCI for short). Yet, now, there was a political void present, and the Italian Communist Party members eagerly hoped to fill it.

Even in northern Italy, where the Germans oversaw a puppet state with the titular figurehead of Mussolini still intact, an underground surge of support for the PCI began to emerge. Despite tremendous German oppression, the Italian communists managed to stage massive strikes in wartime factories and led other forms of revolt against the regime.[i]

Even more consequential, the members of the PCI led the partisan revolt that helped to drive the Germans out of northern Italy altogether. In June 1944, the Allies, with support from the Italian partisans, finally made their way to Rome. Yes, that same month the Allied troops landed in Normandy, the Allies finally breached the gates of Rome itself.

It was a tough slog up the Italian Peninsula from there, with heavily fortified rings of German defenses throughout. The Italian partisans helped make this long march just a little bit easier by attacking the German puppet state of northern Italy from within, as well as from outside. These same partisans helped hunt down and capture a fleeing Benito Mussolini. Italian communist partisans facilitated the infamous execution of Mussolini and his mistress, who had fled with him.[ii] The Allies might not have liked how such things had been executed (for lack of a better word), but they certainly appreciated the helpful thrust of momentum the communists provided in the fight against Italian fascism.

However, this left the door wide open to the West's other great nemesis: communism. The fear of Italy becoming communist would loom large long after the war came to an end in 1945. Nevertheless, for better or for worse, Operation Mincemeat was a stunning success.

---

[i] Williams, Paul. *Operation Gladio: The Unholy Alliance between the Vatican, the CIA, and the Mafia.* 2015. Pg.40.

[ii] Williams, Paul. *Operation Gladio: The Unholy Alliance between the Vatican, the CIA, and the Mafia.* Pg.40.

Conclusion: Falling Hook, Line, and Sinker

The notion that a dead body loaded with fake military documents, along with an entirely fake identity to boot, could be used to trick wartime adversaries seems like the stuff of fiction. These events actually happened in real life, but they make for a good plot in a thriller novel.

British naval officer Duff Cooper, who served as the first lord of the admiralty, apparently thought as much. Even though much of the operation was still unknown to the rest of the world, he published a novel with a glaringly similar premise.

This book was written just a few years after the events of Operation Mincemeat. The book was entitled *Operation Heartbreak*, and anyone involved in Operation Mincemeat could not help but notice the real-life similarities with this supposed "work of fiction."[i] This book highlighted a daring, high-stakes mission that involved the use of a corpse in order to deceive wartime enemies. Either this was a great spark of imaginative creativity on the writer's part, or he was inspired by some rather extraordinary, real-life events.

To give credit where credit is due, there are some great plot twists in the fictional adaptation that are wholly unique. In *Operation Heartbreak*, the main character is not a homeless wanderer but an army veteran who

---

[i] Macintyre, Ben. *Operation Mincemeat: How a Dead Man and a Bizarre Plan Fooled the Nazis and Assured an Allied Victory.* Pg. 672.

longs to serve his country in the wake of World War II. However, he is too old to do so. He gets his wish, though; after he dies from pneumonia, his dead body is put into service in a way that his living one never could.

After this book made the rounds, the people involved in Britain's military intelligence circles became worried. They did not want this fictionalized account to paint their operations in a bad light. In an effort to set the record straight, intelligence operative Ewen Montagu, who had worked quite closely with Operation Mincemeat, came forward to write an official version of events. In 1953, he published a book based on the real-life operation, entitled *The Man Who Never Was*.

This official version of events was actually more popular than the fictionalized account. It was so popular, in fact, that it led to a movie, which was released in 1956. It was largely due to Montagu's book and the subsequent film adaptation that the rest of the world became aware that this strange and daring operation had taken place.

Considering as much, it is worth noting that Operation Mincemeat began with the near intelligence disaster that occurred when an Allied plane crashed in Cádiz, Spain. This plane carried top-secret documents in regard to the Allied invasion plans for French North Africa known as Operation Torch. If the Axis had gained the dates, locations, and other pertinent details about this invasion in advance, it could have been a total disaster for the Allies. And if Operation Torch had failed, it would have ultimately set back the entire Allied war effort.

The Germans did not get to enjoy the benefits of the intelligence that could have been gleaned from the crash at Cádiz, yet the very idea that they *could have* set the wheels in motion for British military intelligence. They began to wonder what could have occurred if the Germans had gotten their hands on the documents at Cádiz. They also speculated if it could be possible to forge fake invasion plan documents. This line of thought led to the planning and execution of a complex and daring counterintelligence operation.

The Germans, with the unwitting assistance of their Spanish contacts, managed to be duped by this grand deception. Call it a lack of due diligence on their part or just plain wishful thinking, but they fell hook, line, and sinker for this bit of skillfully crafted misinformation and deceit, which came to be known as Operation Mincemeat.

If you enjoyed this book, a review on Amazon would be greatly appreciated because it would mean a lot to hear from you.

To leave a review:
1. Open your camera app.
2. Point your mobile device at the QR code.
3. The review page will appear in your web browser.

Thanks for your support!

Here's another book by Captivating History that you might like

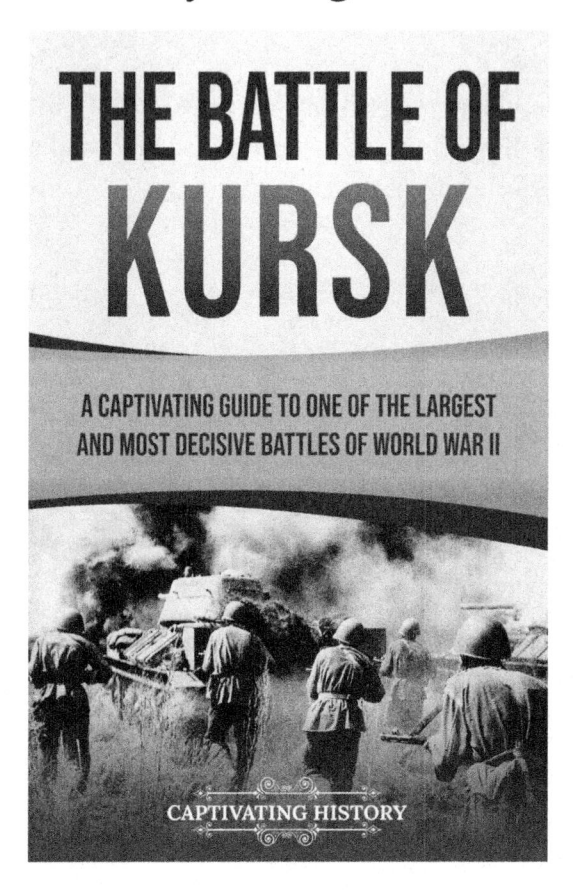

THE BATTLE OF KURSK

A CAPTIVATING GUIDE TO ONE OF THE LARGEST AND MOST DECISIVE BATTLES OF WORLD WAR II

CAPTIVATING HISTORY

Free Bonus from Captivating History (Available for a Limited time)

Hi History Lovers!

Now you have a chance to join our exclusive history list so you can get your first history ebook for free as well as discounts and a potential to get more history books for free!

Simply visit the link below to join.

Or, Scan the QR code!

captivatinghistory.com/ebook

Also, make sure to follow us on Facebook, X, and YouTube by searching for Captivating History.

Further Reading and Reference

Macintyre, Ben. *Operation Mincemeat: How a Dead Man and a Bizarre Plan Fooled the Nazis and Assured an Allied Victory.* 2010.

Williams, Paul. *Operation Gladio: The Unholy Alliance between the Vatican, the CIA, and the Mafia.* 2015.

Image Sources

[1] https://commons.wikimedia.org/wiki/File:Major_Martin.jpg

[2] https://commons.wikimedia.org/wiki/File:UK_National_Archives_-_WO_106;5921.jpg

[3] https://commons.wikimedia.org/wiki/File:The_officers_of_HM_Submarine_SERAPH_on_her_return_to_Portsmouth_after_operations_in_the_Mediterranean,_24_December_1943._A21112.jpg

[4] https://commons.wikimedia.org/wiki/File:Glyndwr_Michael.jpg

Printed in Great Britain
by Amazon